HBF

HELPFUL BOOK FOR
PROFESSIONALS

How to Improve Communication Skills

Improve Communication Skills to Become
a Magnetic Speaker and Draw in Large Crowds!

HBF
EDITORIAL

HOW TO IMPROVE COMMUNICATION SKILLS
Improve Communication Skills to Become
a Magnetic Speaker and Draw in Large Crowds!

© H.B.F. Editorial, 2014
© Charlie A. Fletcher
  Master Resell Rights

ISBN-13: 978-1500994990
ISBN-10: 1500994995

Copyright © 2014 All rights reserved.

Table of Contents

Introduction

Humans need to be speakers in everything that they do, whether they need to convince a girl to go out on a date with them, or to convince a client for a multimillion deal.

Where would we be if not for our communication skills? Here is a Book that helps you to make them better.

CHAPTER 1

Summary

Speaking is a skill that depends on various factors. Now, everyone can speak, as in speak with the mouth, but when we talk about effective speaking, that's a whole different story altogether. Here's what you should know.

Being an Efficient Speaker – Do You Have What it Takes?

Speaking is the best form of communication we know. And we are social beings; we need to communicate with each other constantly. We jabber all the time; it's probably one of the best things we do naturally next to breathing, but when it comes to talking in front of a crowd or talking for a special occasion, such as meeting with an important client, most of us develop frozen cold feet.

This Book deals with teaching you the art of becoming a compelling speaker. But the first step to any education is an awareness of self. Before endeavoring to become a compelling speaker, you must make sure you know what compelling speakers need. Then you must see whether these points are present within you. If not, you must think about improving yourself. Here is what you must know.

Honesty

Honesty is very important when you are looking at talking effectively. Think about it – if you are not convinced about something, how can you convince others? It is not wrong to say that you are not an effective speaker when you are lying. Because you know that something isn't true, you cannot convince other people about it.

Passion

If you are passionate, whatever you say rings true and earnest. Whether you are speaking with a new person, asking him or her out for coffee, or you are speaking on a podium in front of a thousand people, you must make your passion felt.

Knowledge

This strictly applies to public speaking, but you could extrapolate its effectiveness in other areas as well. You must know what you are speaking about. You must always keep enriching your knowledge. Interspersing your knowledge with anecdotes and good examples makes for a more compelling speech.

Making the Connection

Great speakers are those that get their audience involved. This is important whether your audience is sitting across the table with you at a bar sharing a few beers or is listening to you speaking from a stage. You have to get them participate. Asking them questions, making eye contact, gesturing, etc. are some of the ways to do this. On the contrary, if you go droning on, you will never be able to make the connection and your speech will be a total waste.

Be a Good Listener

Effective speakers are constantly listening to others speak. Whether these people are speaking professionally or just speaking to a group of friends, effective speakers will lend an ear to them. They will pick up important things that they say and try to work them into their own speeches whenever the occasion arises.

CHAPTER 2

Summary

Very few people are born orators. Most of them live and learn.

Understanding Your Shortcomings and Overcoming Them – Training Tips

A very essential thing when you are trying to become a successful speaker is to understand where your failings are and improve upon them. In this chapter we are going to see how you can improve yourself as a speaker, whether in a formal or an informal setup.

1. The first step is to understand your failings as a speaker. What happens when you have to speak? Do you become unduly nervous? Do you forget what you have to say? Practicing what you will say beforehand will help. Carrying a small paper with notes on it will also help. Let it be kind of assembly; carrying notes is always permissible. And, if you get nervous, all you have to consider is that people who are listening to you are also just as much human as you are. When you consider this human equality factor, speaking to them does not seem so formidable. In fact, you are the one with the privilege here because you are speaking and these people have actually assembled to hear you speak.

2. If you cannot speak because you think you cannot use the right words, you should not let that deter you. Speakers need not be literary geniuses. You should learn how to work your way around words. You can mug up some quotes that you will speak out. When your quotes are effective, people are already impressed. The Internet has no dearth of quotes.

3. Speak relevantly. That is more important than the language. People want to hear your ideas, not judge you for your knowledge of the language. Hence, when you are preparing anything to say, whether it is a proposal for marriage or a huge business proposal, it is the ideas flowing from you that really matter.

4.   Give anecdotes, but don't go overboard. People always latch on to what you are saying if you can relate that with other living people's experiences. They find your speech more credible.

5.   Most importantly, do not think of yourself as any less than the people that are listening to you. If you know your subject well, don't let anything else get in the way of your speaking.

CHAPTER 3

Summary

It is surprising on how becoming a magnetic speaker actually stands on just three important pegs.

The Three Essentials to Becoming a Magnetic Speaker

Here are the three things that have characterized prominent speakers all through the ages. Learn how to incorporate them into your speaking as well.

The Right Ideas

Whenever you open your mouth to speak, people want to listen to the ideas flowing in your head. Even if you are speaking with a friend about the quality of food at a new restaurant, your friend wants to hear how you find the food to be. Whenever your boss opens his mouth to say something, you want to hear what he wants to say. Get the point? It's the "what you say" part of the conversation that really matters, not the "how you say it." Keep that focus in mind, more so in public speaking. Think of the points that you will be speaking about; it does not really matter if you don't use the best words.

The Right Gestures

Your body language is an important part of you when you are speaking. If you are going to hold yourself stiff, you will come across as too nervous and worked up about what you are going to say. If you hold yourself too loosely, you will come across as an overconfident imp. Hence, you have to strike a balance here. Stand comfortably, but not lazily.

More important are your gestures. Move your hands as you speak, but not too much. Emphasize strong points with a corresponding hand gesture. It makes even the lazy listener sit up and listen.

Always make eye contact with your listeners. Apart from making them feel that you are speaking right to them, you also get an idea of what they are thinking about when you are speaking.

The Right Concentration

Even though it may not seem to be so when you hear them, all effective speakers are extremely concentrated on what they are saying. They put their whole soul into their speech. They are so focused on what they are saying that new points may come to their mind even as they speak. This is how great speeches are made, not by reciting what has been committed to rote memory.

This also includes alertness. Effective speakers are quite astute persons. They are extremely alert about their audience's reactions. A stifled yawn, a bleary look, a rolled eye, nothing goes amiss. They take everything into account and assess how the audience finds what they are saying. They get the idea if the audience does not like something they said. This gives them a chance to justify things a little more, to win the audience over. Or, they can make out if the audience is looking perplexed. If that happens, they try to reiterate the point in a simpler manner.

The bottom line is that you have to be watchful about your audience's feelings. It gives you a chance to keep working up your speech as you say it, to make it sound better to your segment of the audience.

CHAPTER 4

Summary

A speech is a very practical thing. It has to be put into practice and must be practiced.

Practically Practicing Your Speech

Becoming an effective speaker isn't something that you can do overnight. It takes a lot of practice and effort.

It is said that a person who wishes to bowl the audience over with an effective speech must keep practicing the speech 24/7. That isn't wrong actually. But this does not mean you should keep muttering your speech under your breath all the time. The practice that you do refers also to the ideas that you keep thinking about. In fact, if you just remain alert to what's going on around you, it could be effective practice for your speech. That's because by being alert you are being observant – probably something that you see can become an effective anecdote to use in the next speech that you make.

It is also a good idea to have little practice sessions with your family and friends. That doesn't mean you have to bore them with your oratory skills all the time, but you can test the waters subtly. Try saying something to them and see how well you can capture their attention. Try selling them an idea, probably about watching a movie that they aren't much inclined on watching or doing something similar which they are not too keen about. Convincing this small group of people is some practice for your speaking education.

Try more difficult things as you go along. If there is a family gathering or some similar celebration coming along, ask the emcee to give you a shot at the mike. Ask the permission to say something simple and short. It will give you a "feel" of what being in front of an audience could be like. Here you would be at ease because you know more than half the people. Still, an audience always looks forbidding to someone that hasn't had a good deal of speaking experience.

It takes time, but you will become more confident slowly. Remember that confidence is one of the main ingredients of becoming a forceful speaker.

CHAPTER 5

Summary

If you are friends with that stage, nobody can tie your words down.

Coping with the Crowd – Overcoming Stage- Fright

I have a friend who is often asked to speak to crowds. He speaks so much in front of crowds that no one would believe that this guy with the easy swagger on stage is actually scared to death from the prospect of getting up on that stage… even today. What makes him come onstage and deliver all those well-received speeches is that he makes it a point to have two straight shots of vodka a quarter hour before he is scheduled to speak!

Vodka may be one way to overcome stage-fright, but I surely wouldn't recommend that for two reasons. One, it can make you slur if you cannot handle the drink, and two, you may not be able to bring about those improvisation in your speeches that we have spoken about earlier.

So what's the next best option? Read through the following points to learn how you can tackle the problem of stage-fright in the best possible manner.

Make Eye Contact

When you get up on that stage, the first thing you must do is check out the audience. Take a short moment to glance through the audience. Look at every corner, if you can, before you begin. When you see your complete audience, a major part of your intimidation vanishes.

The same applies when you are trying to start speaking something important with someone. If you are confused on how to begin, the first thing to do is to get an eyeful of them. That puts you at ease and you can talk better.

Prepare a Thunderous Opening Line

Practice and re-practice your opening lines well. If you are starting with a quote, try saying that with different tones and modulations and see which works the best. Then go up there and deliver your best.

If you are trying to propose to someone, the same thing works. Have a great opening line ready and give it your best shot.

Any speaker gets twitchy when they have to speak to a new audience. But you must know that this twitchiness lasts for only a few initial seconds. After that, you get into the flow of the talking, considered you have prepared it well, and you don't fumble. Hence, if your opening is well-rehearsed, you will find the nervousness pass away more quickly.

Keep Great Expressions on Your Face

Whatever it takes, don't ever let it show that you are nervous. Keep those smiles coming and don't frown. Speak naturally. When you look back at your speech, your affable expressions makes it look much better.

CHAPTER 6

Summary

If you are not confident about what you speak, you won't come off sounding well to the audience. Here's how to improve your speaking by several notches.

How to Speak Onstage without Hemming and Hawing

To be effective in your speaking, you have to make sure that you speak in a flow. You should not stop midway and make embarrassing pauses while trying to think what you will say next. This is a horrible thing to do when you are onstage, for yourself and your listeners, and when you take one such pause, you feel much more worked up about the whole speech.

The best way to deliver a speech is to say it out in one shot, like it were a big monolog, and not stop midway.

So, how do you do that?

The first important thing you need to be able to speak without flinching midway is to practice your speech well. First of all, commit the speech to memory. Do it the way you like it – either mug up the entire speech or just the points, if you would like to rather work on them as you go. But, the most important practice is the speaking practice. Stand up in your room, and deliver the speech. Do it in front of a mirror. Check yourself as you say it out. You will find a hundred things you can improve on.

When you have said it once, take a pause, and then say it again in front of the mirror. You will see that the faults will have largely reduced. You will be able to speak better too. Doing this a few times really helps.

Psychologists say that people get stage-fright not because they have to deliver a speech or perform on the stage, but because they are too conscious about the way they look and the way they conduct themselves. When you practice in front of a mirror, you can correct most of these problems. In fact, you will become liking the way you conduct yourself after the first few times. This is when the speech will come across more fluently.

Later, get someone to hear you out. Tell them to criticize you openly. Work on these criticisms so that you can do better on stage. It is great if you can ask a few people to hear you delivering your speech because you could get a lot of varied feedback in that manner. Try to remove these faults.

When you are onstage, keep in mind that these are also people like you. Most of them have stage-fright too, and if they were called onstage this very moment, their legs would probably turn to jelly. You are doing a much better job. This boosts your confidence; you are able to speak much better.

CHAPTER 7

Summary

Every speech is delivered because it has to make a point.

Putting Your Point Across

When you are speaking – to a single person or to a complete audience – most of the times, you are trying to make a point. You are trying to see what you are telling. At least, this is very much pronounced when you are speaking onstage. There, you are trying to make hundreds of people see things your way. Hence, it becomes very important to learn how you can put your point across.

We have already spoken a lot about the confidence factor and how you can improve upon it. It is highly important that you use these different methods and improve your confidence so that you can convince those listeners in a better way. If you are of a shaky disposition yourself, no one is going to buy what you are saying, even if it were the voice of reason.

Here are some things you must remember when you are trying to put your point across, especially when you are onstage.

Feel the Audience

A good speaker can do that. Within the first three seconds while they are onstage, they can find out whether they are speaking to a friendly audience or a hostile one. You will have to change your speech accordingly. You won't need major changes, but if the audience is hostile, you might need to put in an example or two more. It is best you prepare for these in advance.

Start Interestingly

Your start should literally glue people onto their seats. It should grab their eyeballs. They must want to listen to you. Begin with an interesting anecdote or quote or example. If you have spoken the same thing someplace else before and it has struck a chord with the audience, then you can use a similar strategy, or even the same thing if you are sure this audience is totally different.

Make Your Point Early On

Some speakers bore their listeners to the verge of death before they come to the main point. A brisk opener is enough to set the right mood. Then go straight to the point. Make the point first and if you have more anecdotes and examples to give, work them in later.

Keep Your Physicality On

Let all those gestures, expressions, eye contact, etc. be on in their full glory. This is what rivets the audience.

CHAPTER 8

Summary

Have you come out of an oration being bowled over by the manner the person spoke? Quite likely, these five essentials were part of their speech.

The Five Essentials of a Dazzling Speech

After checking out hundreds of speakers, some of them of international repute, we have unearthed these five characteristics that are present in all their speeches. Are they present in yours?

The Right Stance

Great speakers hold themselves properly on stage. Their mannerisms are exemplary. Even before they open their mouths to speak something, they have already made an impression because of the way they carry themselves. If you check out some eminent personalities speaking, it will be very easy for you to work these into your speech deliveries too.

The Right Tone

A great speech is varied in tone. The speaker won't drone on and on in the same mode. Their volume will go into an ebb and then surge emphatically when a particular point is of great relevance. They will put the correct emphases on exclamatory marks and questions, which will be found aplenty in the whole body of their speeches anyway.

The Right Interest

One more aspect of great speakers' speeches is that they know how to keep the interest alive. At the slightest hint of the audience losing its interest, they will bring forth a highly interesting point to re-captivate the audience's attention. They will also use interrogations in their speech delivery. These interrogations, if effectively used, will make the listeners ponder if even for just a second. This is what we mean when we speak about "interactive" speeches.

The Right Examples

It is very important to include examples in your speeches if you want to make them attractive. There is one very important point served by this. When you give examples, you are making the speech sound more real, as though what you said has really happened with someone that the listeners know. If you don't give examples, your speech becomes one-dimensional as though it is only your point of view. A good speaker is always looking for great examples to include in future speeches. Keep a small book where you make handy references of such 'examples' as you come by them and use them when needed.

The Right Closing

When you are listening to a speech, you are carried by it, but the part of the speech that really makes a lasting impact is the closing. This is what the people will carry home from the speech in most likelihood. All great speeches are characterized by great closing lines.

CHAPTER 9

Summary

The closing is what lingers in the listeners' mind even after the speech is over. Work on it; this is largely what makes your speech more impactful.

The Most Effective Part of a Magnetic Speech – The Closing

If you make a great speech, but close it in a non-impressive way, a large part of your speech is lost. When you speak effectively, people are very much interested in what you are leading to. People generally have a mindset that makes them think that the best is always saved for the last. That is the reason they are very much eager to hear the close of the speech. Now, if you don't work on it, your speech will become a completely lost cause.

Here are different ways in which you can effectively bring your speech to an effective climax.

1. Pose a question at the end. This question should have to do with what you have just said. Keep the question a little tough, a question whose answer won't come right away into their minds. However, the question must make them go back on what you have said and scout for the answer. Effective speakers are known to use this little device which makes their speeches remain in the listeners' minds for a long time even after they are long over.

2. Place a great quote at the end. Spend time to search for such quotes on the Internet or elsewhere and speak them with aplomb. Do not elaborate on these quotes; leave them hanging in the minds of the audience.

3. Sum it all up at the end. If you don't know how to effectively close your speech, just give them a summary. This helps too, because it gives you a chance to reinforce what you just said on your audiences' minds.

4. If you have something to give away, keep that announcement at the end. This is a great way to get people interested in what you have been

saying. After you have made the announcement for the giveaway, summarize the main parts of your speech.

5.   Make an earnest plea. This works if your speech is for a clause.

Or, get someone else – an eminent personality, if possible – to come ahead and make the plea. Just hand over the mike to them and move offstage.

These are various ways in which you can bring your speech to an effective close. Time and again, it has been proven that any and all of these methods work.

CHAPTER 10

Summary

A speaker is always a listener, a student.

Improving Yourself as a Speaker

A speaker is always a student. You have to always keep learning. You can never say that you have become the most perfect speaker there is. Speaking is such a personal thing that there is a great deal of variety in this realm. Even as you listen to other people speaking – by being a part of a live audience or checking them out on television – you see that there are so many of their impressive things that you can include in your speeches. There is definitely no harm in trying out. You could try working in these traits in your own delivery and improve.

A speaker is also a much-informed person. Keep yourself abreast of what's going on. You will have to allude to anything, anytime in your speeches. You can speak the most relevant speeches at any time if you are abreast of what's happening.

Also, speak with people. Take their feedback on everything. Use this in your speeches. This is general feedback, general opinion. It is always great to put a joke about what people are already making jokes. It helps. The speech becomes more colorful.

Keep yourself educated on great quotes too, at least those quotes that are effective for your subject. But remember that all the great quotes will already have been taken, other speakers might have used it. Your audience might have heard those speeches. So, try to keep your quotes as unique as possible.

Most importantly, keep yourself aware of human nature at all times. People who are listening to you are human entities. They will react as people normally do. If you learn how to read people and their faces, you will do better at creating an impact with the speeches that you deliver.

Conclusion

Speaking is an enjoyable activity once you get the hang of it.

Go on, conquer the microphone and your audience.

You have what you need now.

All the best!!! You have what you need now.

All the best!!!